I Was Born When the Sap Runs

As told by
Randall Weber

This is a true story about the maple sugaring season in New Hampshire.

Dedicated to my Dad

I was born in late March. Daddy says he found me as a baby in a sap bucket. I know babies may be sweet, but they do not come in sap buckets.

In late winter, Dad and I go out and check th[e] lines on the trees to make sure they are tigh[t] and clean inside.

On the first warm, sunny days of March,
go out and hang buckets close to our house
and listen for the familiar plink, plunk of
the sap dripping into the metal buckets.
It is music to my ears.

Sometimes I taste the sap as it drops from the trees into the buckets. It tastes so sweet.

Sometimes, I find an icicle in the morning where the sap has frozen. I suck on the sweet icicles as I wait for my bus. Mmmmmmmm...

By the time I get home from school, it is time to collect the sap if the day has been warm and not too windy. I go with my dad and pump the sap from the collection buckets on the trees with lines.

It is fun riding on the back roads and seeing the first signs of spring. I keep my eye out for the first robin.

Mom and I usually collect the sap buckets on the trees near the house with my red wagon. Friends like to help, too. We gather the sap and pour it into a big collection tank outside the sugar house.

When we have enough sap collected, Dad lets me start the fire in the evaporator's stove.

We keep the fire really hot under the sap, which means burning lots of wood that I helped Dad split during the summer months.

Then, we watch for the sap to boil and reach that magic temperature where sap turns to syrup.

I always know that friends and neighbors will be stopping by to taste the warm, sweet syrup that Dad draws off from the evaporator.

At night when Dad boils, I sit by the glow of the evaporator's fire with fresh maple syrup poured over vanilla ice cream and dream about riding my bike again.

Soon buds will be out on the trees
and the sugaring season will be over for
another year...

...but we'll have lots of syrup for my pancakes and my milk until the next time he sap runs and I will be another year older.

Randall Weber is the only NH native in his family. Randall has grown up having syrup on his pancakes, but also loves it in his milk and on ice cream.